abolish work

"Abolish Restaurants"
plus
"Work, Community, Politics, War"
prole.info

Abolish Work
Prole.info

© PM Press 2014
All rights reserved. No part of this book may be transmitted by any
means without permission in writing from the publisher.

PM Press
PO Box 23912
Oakland, CA 94623
www.pmpress.org

Copublished with:
thoughtcrime ink
C/O Black Cat Press
4508 118 Avenue
Edmonton, Alberta T5W 1A9
www.thoughtcrimeink.com

ISBN: 978-1-60486-340-6
Library of Congress Control Number: 2013956928

10 9 8 7 6 5 4 3 2

Printed in the USA, by the Employee Owners of Thomson-Shore in
Dexter, Michigan.
www.thomsonshore.com

abolish work

prole.info

contents

1   **Abolish Restaurants**
    A Worker's Critique of the Food Service Industry

2   Foreword

        HOW A RESTAURANT IS SET UP:
6   What Is a Restaurant?
10   The Production Process
16   Division of Labor and Use of Machines
22   Intensity and Stress
24   Tips
26   Customers
30   Coercion and Competition

        HOW A RESTAURANT IS TAKEN APART:
36   What the Worker Wants
40   Work Groups
44   Workers, Management, and Worker-Management
48   Unions
52   A World Without Restaurants

57   **Capitalist Society**

61   **Work   Community   Politics   War**

abolish restaurants
a worker's critique of the food service industry

"When one comes to think of it, it is strange that thousands of people in a great modern city should spend their waking hours swabbing dishes in hot dens underground. The question I am raising is why this life goes on—what purpose it serves, and who wants it to continue . . ."

George Orwell

Your back hurts from standing up for 6, 10, or 14 hours in a row. You reek of seafood and steak spices. You've been running back and forth all night. You're hot. Your clothes are sticking to you with sweat. All sorts of strange thoughts come into your head.

You catch bits and pieces of customers' conversations, while having constantly interrupted ones with your co-workers.

"Oh isn't it nice, this restaurant gives money to that save-the-wolves charity."

"I can't believe she slept with him. What a slut!"

"Yeah, the carpenters are giving us problems. They want more money."

"So he says to me, 'I think my escargots are bad,' and I say 'What do you expect? They're snails' AHAHAHAHAHAHAH."

No time to worry about relationship problems, or whether you fed your cat this morning, or how you're going to make rent this month, a new order is up.

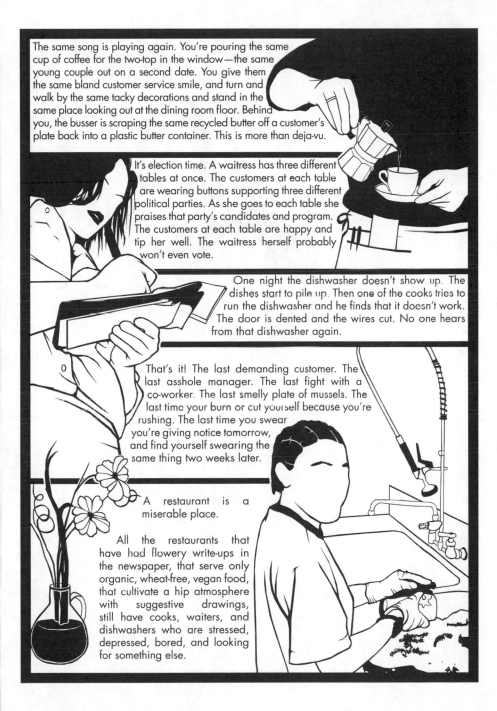

The same song is playing again. You're pouring the same cup of coffee for the two-top in the window—the same young couple out on a second date. You give them the same bland customer service smile, and turn and walk by the same tacky decorations and stand in the same place looking out at the dining room floor. Behind you, the busser is scraping the same recycled butter off a customer's plate back into a plastic butter container. This is more than deja-vu.

It's election time. A waitress has three different tables at once. The customers at each table are wearing buttons supporting three different political parties. As she goes to each table she praises that party's candidates and program. The customers at each table are happy and tip her well. The waitress herself probably won't even vote.

One night the dishwasher doesn't show up. The dishes start to pile up. Then one of the cooks tries to run the dishwasher and he finds that it doesn't work. The door is dented and the wires cut. No one hears from that dishwasher again.

That's it! The last demanding customer. The last asshole manager. The last fight with a co-worker. The last smelly plate of mussels. The last time your burn or cut yourself because you're rushing. The last time you swear you're giving notice tomorrow, and find yourself swearing the same thing two weeks later.

A restaurant is a miserable place.

All the restaurants that have had flowery write-ups in the newspaper, that serve only organic, wheat-free, vegan food, that cultivate a hip atmosphere with suggestive drawings, still have cooks, waiters, and dishwashers who are stressed, depressed, bored, and looking for something else.

HOW A RESTAURANT IS SET UP

"You can't make an omelette without breaking a few eggs."

Maximilien Robespierre

WHAT IS A RESTAURANT?

"There's no such thing as a free lunch."

popularized by
Milton Friedman

Today it's hard to imagine a world without restaurants. The conditions that create restaurants are everywhere and seem almost natural. We have trouble even thinking how people could feed each other in any other way (besides going to the grocery store of course). But restaurants as much as parliamentary democracy, the state, nationalism, or professional police are an invention of the modern capitalist world.

The first restaurants began to appear in Paris in the 1760s, and even as late as the 1850s the majority of all the restaurants in the world were located in Paris. At first they sold only small meat stews, called *"restaurants"* that were meant to restore health to sick people.

A. Boulanger

Before that, people didn't go out to eat as they do today. Aristocrats had servants, who cooked for them. And the rest of the population, who were mainly peasant farmers, ate meals at home. There were inns for travelers, where meals were included in the price of the room, and the innkeeper and his lodgers would sit and eat together at the same table. There were caterers who would prepare or host meals for weddings, funerals, and other special occasions. There were taverns, wineries, cafés, and bakeries where specific kinds of food and drink could be consumed on the premises. But there were no restaurants.

Partially this was because restaurants would have been illegal. Food was made by craftsmen organized into a number of highly specialized guilds. There were the *"charcutiers"* (who made sausages and pork), the *"rôtisseurs"* (who prepared roasted meats and poultry), the pâté-makers, the gingerbread-makers, the vinegar-makers, the pastry cooks. By law only a master gingerbread-maker could make gingerbread, and everyone else was legally forbidden to make gingerbread. At best, a particular family or group of craftsmen could get the king's permission to produce and sell a few different categories of food.

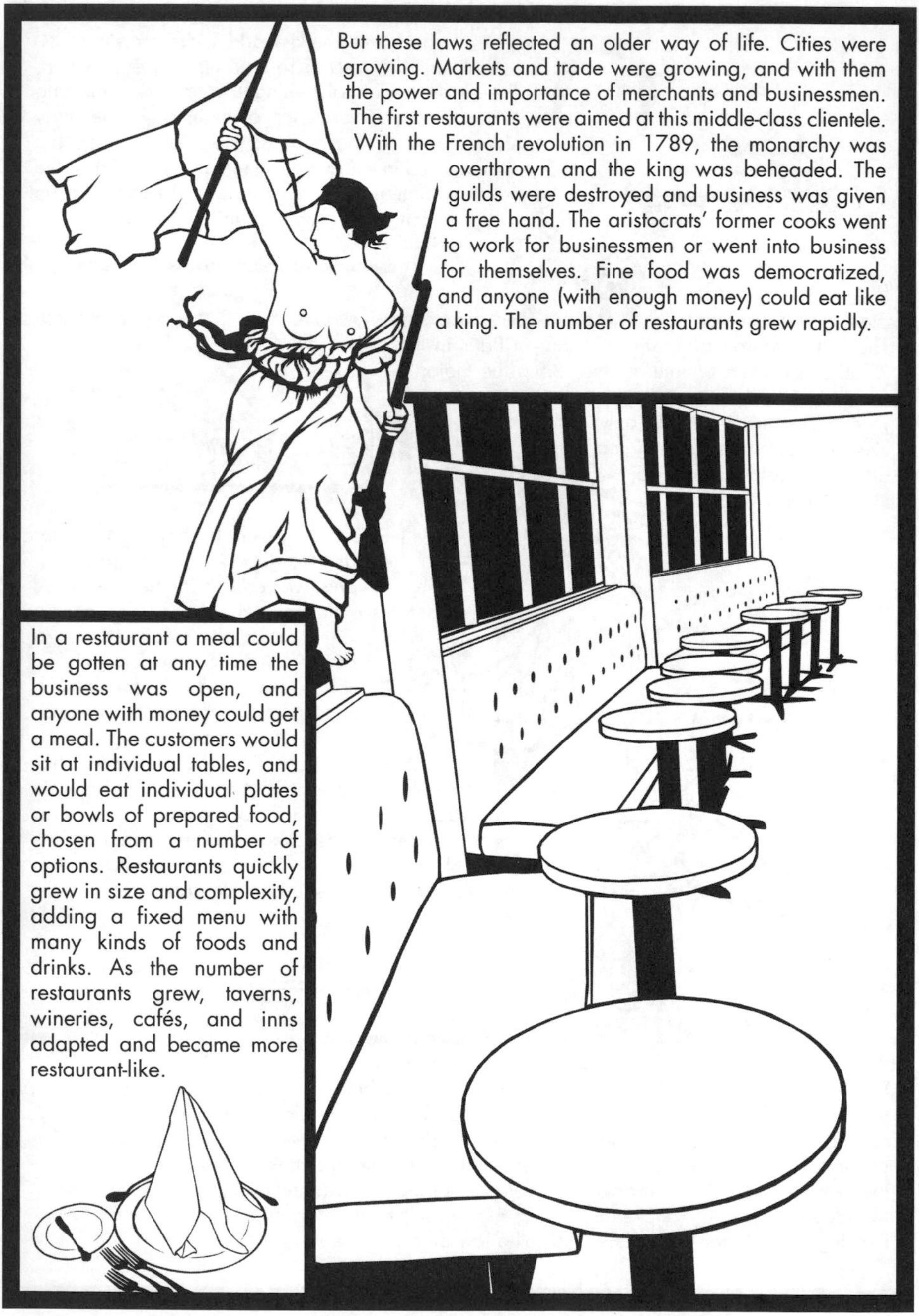
But these laws reflected an older way of life. Cities were growing. Markets and trade were growing, and with them the power and importance of merchants and businessmen. The first restaurants were aimed at this middle-class clientele. With the French revolution in 1789, the monarchy was overthrown and the king was beheaded. The guilds were destroyed and business was given a free hand. The aristocrats' former cooks went to work for businessmen or went into business for themselves. Fine food was democratized, and anyone (with enough money) could eat like a king. The number of restaurants grew rapidly.
In a restaurant a meal could be gotten at any time the business was open, and anyone with money could get a meal. The customers would sit at individual tables, and would eat individual plates or bowls of prepared food, chosen from a number of options. Restaurants quickly grew in size and complexity, adding a fixed menu with many kinds of foods and drinks. As the number of restaurants grew, taverns, wineries, cafés, and inns adapted and became more restaurant-like.

The growth of the restaurant was the growth of the market. Needs that were once fulfilled either through a direct relationship of domination (between a lord and his servants) or a private relationship (within the family), were now fulfilled on the open market. What was once a direct oppressive relationship now became the relationship between buyer and seller. A similar expansion of the market took place over a century later with the rise of fast food. As the 1950s housewife was undermined and women moved into the open labor market, many of the tasks that had been done by women in the house were transferred onto the market. Fast food restaurants grew rapidly, and paid wages for what used to be housework.

The 19th century brought the industrial revolution. Machinery was revolutionizing the way everything was made. As agricultural production methods got more efficient, peasants were driven off the land and joined the former craftsmen in the cities as the modern working class. They had no way to make money but to work for someone else.

Sometime in the 19th century, the modern restaurant crystallized in the form we know it today, and spread all over the globe. This required several things: businessmen with capital to invest in restaurants, customers who expected to satisfy their need for food on the open market, by buying it, and workers, with no way to live but by working for someone else. As these conditions developed, so did restaurants.

THE PRODUCTION PROCESS

"Money is like an arm or a leg—use it or lose it."

Henry Ford

The customers see in a restaurant a meal—prepared food to be eaten on the premises. They also see a place to go out and socialize—a semi-public place, a place to do business, to celebrate one's birthday, to take a date. Customers buy food, but they also buy atmosphere, culture, the experience of a restaurant meal. Customers like restaurants. They are the consumers.

The restaurant owner is the seller. They are really in charge of the production process, and what they have for sale tends to shape the demand of the customers. The restaurant owner isn't in business out of a desire to feed people. They're in it to make money. Maybe the owner was a chef or a waiter who worked his way up. Maybe he was born into money and has no background in restaurant work. In any case, when they go into business for themselves, restaurant owners want one thing: to make money.

They buy ovens, refrigerators, pots, pans, glasses, napkins, knives, cutting boards, silverware, tables, chairs, wine, liquor, cleaning equipment, raw and canned foods, oils, spices, and everything else that is needed to run a modern restaurant. The value of these things is determined by the amount of work time necessary to make them. As they are used up, that value makes its way into the value of a restaurant meal.

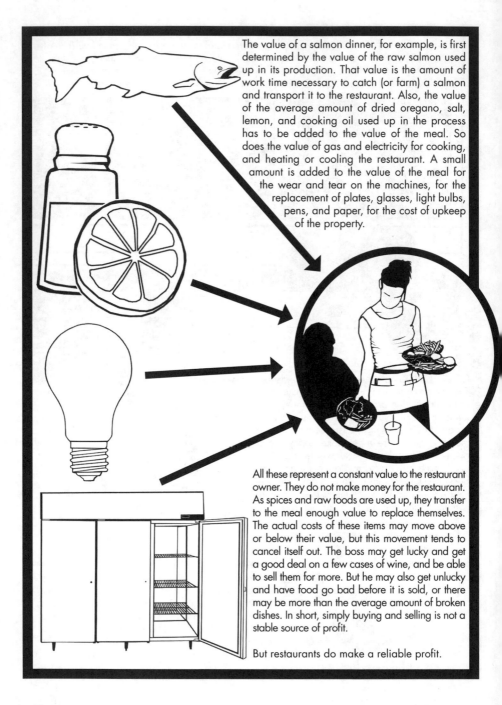

The value of a salmon dinner, for example, is first determined by the value of the raw salmon used up in its production. That value is the amount of work time necessary to catch (or farm) a salmon and transport it to the restaurant. Also, the value of the average amount of dried oregano, salt, lemon, and cooking oil used up in the process has to be added to the value of the meal. So does the value of gas and electricity for cooking, and heating or cooling the restaurant. A small amount is added to the value of the meal for the wear and tear on the machines, for the replacement of plates, glasses, light bulbs, pens, and paper, for the cost of upkeep of the property.

All these represent a constant value to the restaurant owner. They do not make money for the restaurant. As spices and raw foods are used up, they transfer to the meal enough value to replace themselves. The actual costs of these items may move above or below their value, but this movement tends to cancel itself out. The boss may get lucky and get a good deal on a few cases of wine, and be able to sell them for more. But he may also get unlucky and have food go bad before it is sold, or there may be more than the average amount of broken dishes. In short, simply buying and selling is not a stable source of profit.

But restaurants do make a reliable profit.

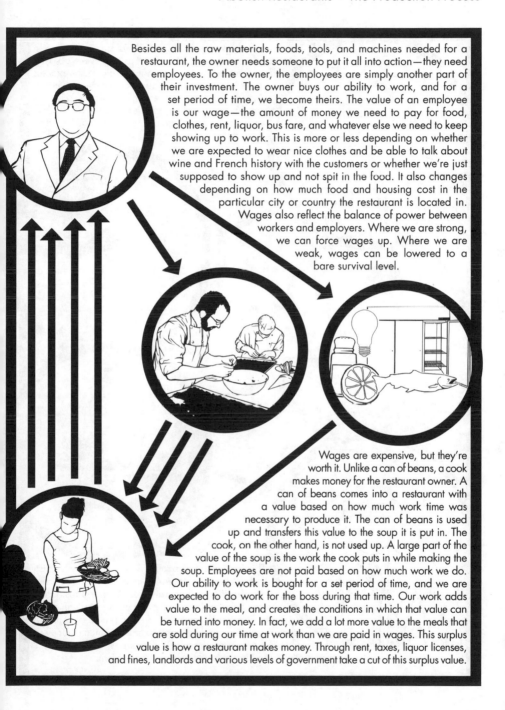

Besides all the raw materials, foods, tools, and machines needed for a restaurant, the owner needs someone to put it all into action—they need employees. To the owner, the employees are simply another part of their investment. The owner buys our ability to work, and for a set period of time, we become theirs. The value of an employee is our wage—the amount of money we need to pay for food, clothes, rent, liquor, bus fare, and whatever else we need to keep showing up to work. This is more or less depending on whether we are expected to wear nice clothes and be able to talk about wine and French history with the customers or whether we're just supposed to show up and not spit in the food. It also changes depending on how much food and housing cost in the particular city or country the restaurant is located in. Wages also reflect the balance of power between workers and employers. Where we are strong, we can force wages up. Where we are weak, wages can be lowered to a bare survival level.

Wages are expensive, but they're worth it. Unlike a can of beans, a cook makes money for the restaurant owner. A can of beans comes into a restaurant with a value based on how much work time was necessary to produce it. The can of beans is used up and transfers this value to the soup it is put in. The cook, on the other hand, is not used up. A large part of the value of the soup is the work the cook puts in while making the soup. Employees are not paid based on how much work we do. Our ability to work is bought for a set period of time, and we are expected to do work for the boss during that time. Our work adds value to the meal, and creates the conditions in which that value can be turned into money. In fact, we add a lot more value to the meals that are sold during our time at work than we are paid in wages. This surplus value is how a restaurant makes money. Through rent, taxes, liquor licenses, and fines, landlords and various levels of government take a cut of this surplus value.

The entrepreneur starts with money. He buys commodities (foods, spices, machines, and tools, as well as employees' ability to work). These are set in motion in the production process and create a commodity—the restaurant meal—which is sold immediately to customers on site. This money is more than the original investment. It is then re-invested and the circuit starts all over again. By getting his capital to flow through the production process, that capital grows.

£ € ¥ $

Money

Commodities

Production

Commodities worth more

more **M**oney

This movement of capital is why restaurants exist, and it gives restaurants their particular shapes and priorities. What matters is not that a restaurant produces food, but that it produces surplus value and profit. The restaurant is a production process that makes the boss money, and he wants to make as much money as possible. Time and again safety, cleanliness, and even legal considerations are thrown aside to make more profit.

The restaurant represents something very different to the workers. Those who work in a restaurant don't do it because we want to. We are forced to. We have no other way to make a living but to sell our ability to work to someone else—and it might as well be a restaurant owner. We don't make food because we like to make food or because we want to make food for this or that particular customer. When cleaning the floors or opening wine bottles, we aren't fulfilling a need for some kind of meaningful activity. We are simply trading our time for a wage. That is what the restaurant represents to us.

Our time and activity in the restaurant is not our own—it belongs to management. Although everything in the restaurant is put into motion and works only because we make it work, the restaurant is something outside and against us. The harder we work, the more money the restaurant makes. The less we are paid, the more money the restaurant makes. It is rare that the workers in a restaurant can afford to eat regularly at the restaurant they work in. It is common for restaurant workers to carry plates of exquisite food around all night, while having nothing but coffee and bread in our stomachs. A restaurant can't function without workers, but there is a constant conflict between the workers and the work. Simply standing up for ourselves makes us fight against the production process. We catch our breath during a dinner rush and slow down the production of a meal. We steal food, cut corners, or just stand and talk, and in the process cut into production. The boss, who represents the production process, is constantly enforcing it on us. We are yelled at if we're not doing anything or if we're not doing something faster than humanly possible or if we make mistakes that slow down money-making. We come to hate the work and to hate the boss. The struggle between restaurant workers and restaurant management is just as much a part of restaurants as the food, wine, tables, chairs, or check presenters.

prole.info

DIVISION OF LABOR
AND THE USE OF MACHINES

"The real danger is not that machines will begin to think like men, but that men will begin to think like machines."

Sydney J. Harris

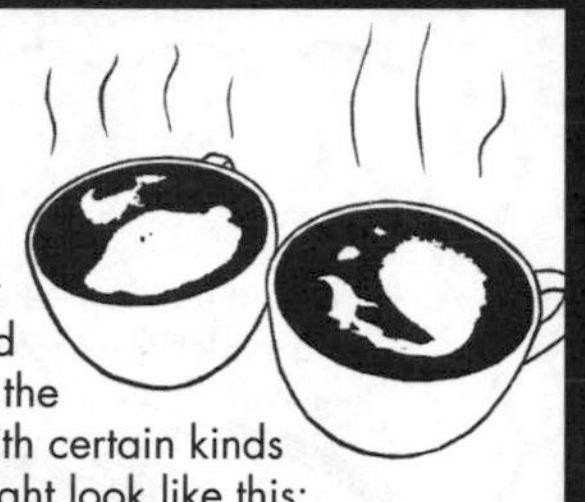

In order for restaurants to make as much money as efficiently as possible, they tend to be organized in similar ways.

Tasks are divided up, and different workers specialize in different aspects of the work. These divisions develop because they allow us to pump out meals quicker. The first and most obvious divisions are between management and workers, and between "front of the house" and "back of the house." As the divisions become solidified, they are ranked and associated with certain kinds of people. The division of labor in a typical small restaurant might look like this:

management

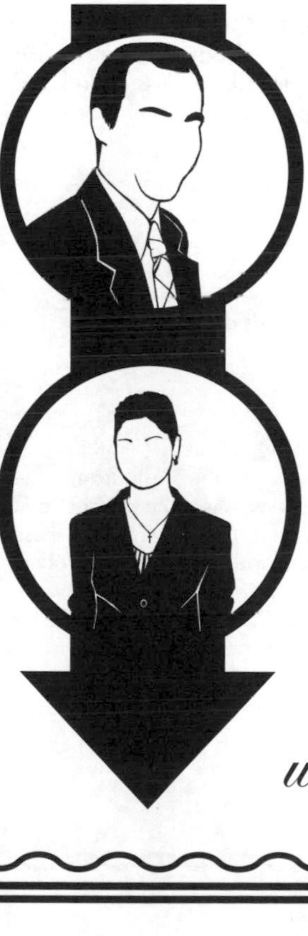

THE BOSS

(Owns the restaurant. His job is to make sure the restaurant is making money. Usually knows a lot about food. He sets the menu, buys equipment, hires and fires people, and sometimes walks around to make sure everyone is working as hard as possible. The restaurant is his capital.)

THE MANAGER

(Her job is to practically oversee the employees. She deals with complaints and problems as they arise, making sure the work process is running smoothly. Often she is older than the other employees, and has worked as a waitress, bartender, or cook for many years. While she is the enforcer of the production process, she doesn't directly profit from it, and is therefore not as enthusiastic an enforcer as the boss. Sometimes the role of the manager is combined with that of the bartender, the headwaiter, or the senior cook.)

workers

back of the house

It is common for the entire back of the house to be illegal immigrants getting paid under the table. They don't have any contact with the customers and therefore don't have to look like or speak the same language as the customers.

HOT COOK
(Prepares hot foods—mainly entrées. Usually the best-paid employee in the kitchen, and sometimes has some supervisory role.)

COLD COOK
(Prepares salads, side orders, and desserts. Slightly less skilled and less paid than the hot cook.)

PREP COOK
(Prepares ingredients. Makes some bulk foods like sauces and soups. Moves foods around and helps other cooks during rushes.)

DISHWASHER
(The lowest job in the restaurant. The dishwasher just washes the dishes and moves them around. They have the smelliest, loudest, hottest, and most physical job in the restaurant. They are usually the worst paid as well. This job is usually reserved for the very young or the very old.)

front of the house

The front of the house is expected to look presentable, and be able to deal with customers. Often are educated, and have useless college degrees in things like "English," "History," or—worse yet—"Art History."

BARTENDER
(Makes drinks for customers at the bar and for the waiters. Has to be able to appear to know a lot about mixed drinks, beers, and wines. Sells some food.)

SERVERS
(Takes orders, serves food, takes payment, and generally sells as much as possible. Have to be able to appear to know a lot about the food and something about the drinks.)

HOSTESS
(Answers the phone and seats customers. Usually only is needed full-time in large restaurants, and in smaller ones only on weekends and holidays. Hostesses are almost always women.)

BUSSER
(Clears away dirty dishes. Cleans and resets tables. Also does some food prep, like cutting bread and pouring water. Doesn't have to talk to the customers very much.)

The bussers and hostesses usually want to "move up" and be a server or a bartender, just as the dishwasher wants to cook, the prep cook wants to be a cold cook and the cold cook wants to be a hot cook.

The actual job descriptions vary widely between restaurants, as do the ages, genders, and ethnicities associated with them. Still, in most restaurants, the boss has an idea of the kind of person he wants to do each job. The division of labor is overlaid with cultural divisions.

The work process is chopped up into little pieces. Each part is the responsibility of a different worker. This is very efficient for the purpose of making money. We repeat the same specialized tasks over and over again and get very good at them. At the same time, the work loses any meaning it ever had for us. Even those who decided to get a job in a restaurant (as opposed to some other shit job) because they have some interest in food or wine, quickly lose that interest. The same fifteen minutes (or hour-and-a-half) seem to repeat themselves over and over again, day after day. The work becomes second nature. On a good day we can fly through it almost unconsciously, on a bad day we are painfully aware of how boring and pointless it is.

Compared to most other areas of the economy, restaurants are very labor-intensive. Still, just as the production process tends to increase the division of labor, it also tends to push the use of machines. Every modern restaurant has some machines (stoves, refrigerators, coffee machines, etc.), but there is a definite tendency to increase the use of machinery. A cook can boil water for tea easily enough on the stove, but it is quicker and easier to have a machine with near-boiling water ready all the time. A waiter can write down orders and hand them to the kitchen, but that same waiter can take even more orders in less time if he doesn't have to write them down and walk into a kitchen, and instead just punches them into a computer, which sends them into the kitchen.

We tend to grow attached to the objects we work with. We like a good wine key, a good spatula, or a nice sharp knife because they make it a little easier to do our work. We hate when the computer system goes down, because then we have to do everything by hand. Whether they're working well or not, the machines impose a rhythm on our work. The job of making a particular entrée may be dictated by how long the oven takes to cook one ingredient, how long the microwave takes to heat up another. Even in a rush we have to wait by the credit card machine while it's slowly printing out. On a good day, the machines in a restaurant aren't noticed. On a bad day we can spend all night cursing them.

Usually, the larger the restaurant, the more chopped-up the work process is, and the stronger the tendency is to use machines to replace tasks done by people. In a very small restaurant, the jobs of the waiter, bartender, busser, and hostess may combine into one. In a very large restaurant, the tasks of the waiter may be split between two or three different job descriptions. Similarly, the use of machines to replace human tasks tends to be limited in smaller restaurants, and tends to be greater in larger ones with more capital.

Machines are not used to make our jobs easier. They are used as a way to increase the amount of product a particular worker can pump out in a given amount of time. The first restaurants to introduce a new machine are very profitable, because they are able to produce more efficiently than the industry average. At the same time, the machines (like the food or the spices) do not make money for the restaurant—only the employees do. As new machines become widely used, it becomes merely inefficient not to have one. The machines replace human tasks. They become just another link in the chain of tasks. We don't have less work to do. We just have to do a smaller range of tasks, more often. Our job becomes even more specialized and repetitive. And we get angry at the machines when they don't do their part of the job. Our activity at work has been reduced to such a mechanical level that we can come into conflict with the machines.

The restaurant is itself a small part of the division of labor within the economy. The process of getting food on the table is chopped into pieces. The restaurant is only the last part of the process, where the food is prepared and sold to the customers. The raw meat and fish, the canned food and spices, the tables, chairs, napkins, and aprons all come into the restaurant as the finished commodities of other enterprises. They are produced by workers in a similar production process and under similar conditions. As restaurant workers, we are cut off from these workers. We only see the sales representative of the wine distribution company, as he samples wines with the boss, or the deliveryman for the laundry company as he picks up or drops off the sacks of napkins and tablecloths.

INTENSITY AND STRESS

"If you can't stand the heat, get out of the kitchen."

Harry S. Truman

A restaurant is different from other industries in that its product cannot really be stored and sold later. Unlike a car factory or a construction site, a restaurant produces a meal which has to be consumed within a few minutes of its production or it can't be sold. This means that the work can't be done in a steady rhythm. It comes in waves and rushes, with slow times in between. Restaurant workers are either bored or stressed. We're either trying to look busy, with nothing to do, or trying not to fall hopelessly behind, doing ten things at once.

Everyone who works in a restaurant is pushed to work harder and faster. The boss has an interest in getting more work out of the same number of employees or in getting the same amount of work out of fewer employees. We are pushed to ridiculous extremes. During a typical dinner rush you will see a cook frying french fries, keeping an eye on a steak on the grill, waiting for a soup to come out of the microwave, boiling pasta, heating up sauce in a pan, and seasoning some vegetables, all at once. At the same time, a waitress carrying four coffees and a dessert menu to one table stops and takes a drink order from another and tells two more tables that she'll be there in just a minute. We are pushed to do more and more very precise tasks at once and in rapid succession, and yelled at when we don't get it right. The one thing that the workers of almost every restaurant are given for free is coffee, which helps us speed up to the insane pace of the work during rushes. The pace is set by the amount of work there is to do. We have to adjust ourselves to that pace whether we're sick, hung-over, tired, or just distracted thinking about something else. We superglue shut our cuts and continue on.

The stress of the rushes gets to everyone in a restaurant. Almost all the workers dip into the wine, whiskey, and tequila when the boss's back is turned. Quite a few employees get drunk or high immediately after work. And after any typical night everyone is exhausted. On our way home from work, we notice that our back, our knees, or our fingers hurt. When we go to sleep we hope we won't dream about forgetting an order or being yelled at by the boss.

TIPS

"Waitressing is the number one occupation for female non-college graduates in this country. It's the one job basically any woman can get and make a living on. The reason is because of tips."

Mr. White
(from the movie "Reservoir Dogs")

Many restaurant workers make tips. This means that part of our wage is paid directly by the boss, and part is paid by the customer. Tipped jobs are often the better paid jobs in the restaurant. This creates a false association for some people between tips and good pay. Tipping is a pay structure set up by the boss for very specific purposes.

today's over-priced special:

POUTINE
GUMBO
PO' BOYS
mayonnaise extra

Restaurants can't produce in an even assembly-line rhythm like some industries, because meals have to be eaten right away. In fact, most of a meal can't even be started until there is a ready buyer sitting in the restaurant. This means that the ups and downs of regular business hit restaurants particularly hard. When employees are paid in tips, our wage is tied to sales. This means that when business is good, the boss makes a little less profit than he would be if he paid us a steady wage because our wages are a little higher. When business is bad, he makes a little more because our wages are lower. It is a way of transferring some of the risks of entrepreneurship off the boss and onto the workers.

More importantly, workers whose wages are made up largely of tips are schizophrenic. Waiters (who usually make tips) don't like work any more than cooks (who don't usually make tips). It is just as meaningless, stressful, and alienating for both of them. At the same time, cooks make the same wage whether business is good or bad. They just have to work harder when business is good. Waiters make more when business is good, and therefore have an interest in pushing themselves and other employees harder—which of course makes more money for the boss as well. This function of tips is paralleled throughout the economy. Steelworkers' pensions are tied to the company's stock, and workers in a coffee shop are given shares in the company they work for.

Also, tips re-enforce the division of labor. Tips usually flow from the top down. The customer has a certain amount of power over the waiter, since she can decide to tip him more or less. It's not uncommon for some yuppie customer to sit for a minute, looking at the bill, and then at the waiter, relishing that moment of power. At the end of the night, the waiter then tips out of his tips to other employees, such as the busser or hostess. He too can tip out more or less within certain limits. The flow of tips from top to bottom re-enforces the hierarchy in the restaurant. This last function of tipping can be lessened in restaurants where tips are pooled.

CUSTOMERS

"The customer is always right."

H. Gordon Selfridge

For the most part, restaurant workers hate restaurant customers. When we run into other people who work customer service jobs at the bar or at a party, we can tell stories and rant about customers for hours.

In most restaurants, the workers could not afford to eat at the restaurant on a regular basis. This means that we tend to be serving people who are better off than we are, even if they aren't necessarily rich bastards. But this is only the background for the resentment of the customers. Customers can easily be working class people with jobs just as alienating and miserable as restaurant work. Even someone who works 60 hours a week as a busser may go out to eat and be an asshole customer. The class background of the customers is less important than their position as customers in a restaurant.

The customers are the buyers. They think they're buying good food and good service. What they get more often is the appearance of good food and good service. Restaurant food is rarely as fresh or clean as homemade food. The loud, obnoxious customer will have their coffee refilled with decaf. We'll tell the customers we're out of something if we're too busy to get it for them. We'll recommend the food that is the most expensive or the easiest to prepare.

The customers aren't used to the production process. A large part of the job of the front-end staff is to fit them efficiently into that process. We get good at getting them to order, eat, and pay when we want them to. The best waiters are those that can get a large amount of tables at once to order a lot of food and drinks, to eat them and pay quickly and to make them think they're ordering, eating, and paying at their own pace. This is possible because the whole meal is streamlined, with a limited number of options. If they want their meal prepared a special way or if they're not ready to order or pay when we stop at their table, they are causing more work for us. We start to develop not-entirely-inaccurate prejudices based on what kinds of customers are going to be difficult to fit into the rhythm of production or which customers will tip well. Old people and kids are trouble. Foreign tourists and businessmen don't tip well. Construction workers and of course other restaurant workers generally do.

Customers have a lot of power over the restaurant workers—and not just when they tip us. A bad comment card can get us yelled at. A serious complaint to the manager could get us fired. The imbalance of power is such that customers sometimes act like little bosses. They can be demanding, rude, drunken assholes, but we have to be nice to them, and it's our job to make them happy. We hate them for the power they have over us. They form part of the surveillance apparatus of the restaurant.

We have the same careful conversations with customers over and over again. We learn to read them quickly and to say what they want to hear. We flirt and use worn-out jokes to get them to buy a lot, eat quickly, and tip well. But when we step away from the table, or out of earshot, the polite customer service face quickly drops off.

We curse them, or laugh about them, or talk about which ones we'd like to fuck, or wonder if that's a father and daughter or a businessman and his mistress. We take a strange kind of pleasure in this two-facedness. In the oppressive customer service atmosphere it is almost rebellious.

Customers are also a restaurant's weakness. The restaurant is dependent on them. A customer may complain to management, but they may also take our side. Customers have direct contact with restaurant workers, and usually want to imagine that these workers are happy and well-treated. We can sometimes use them as a way to put pressure on management. A picket line in front of a restaurant turns away customers far easier than a picket line in front of a shipyard keeps shipping companies from using it.

COERCION AND COMPETITION

"We run up against the upholders of order, but we also keep running up against each other on a much more everyday level. This is the reality of capitalism."

Dominique Karamazov

In a restaurant this happens literally. When we're running around trying to get ten things done at once, we're bound to bump into each other occasionally. The more people that can be sat in the restaurant at a given time, the more money the boss can make. This means that in all but the finest restaurants there is a tendency to pack tables close together in the dining room and to make the kitchen and the workstations for the bussers and waiters as small as possible. This multiplies the amount of collisions as well as the potential for us to drop plates, or hurt each other. We are constantly in each other's face, whether we like it or not.

The boss sets up a restaurant as a way to make money. But the workers, who are essential to the production process, are hostile to it. This means that in order for production to be kept up, employees have to be constantly coerced, monitored, and played off against one another.

Management is always watching to make sure we are doing our job. The boss or the manager is there, telling us to work harder, faster, more . . . If you don't, your job could be in danger. Depending on the size of the restaurant this can be as personal as an abusive father or as impersonal as a police state. They assume (correctly) that employees will steal when no one is looking, and are constantly doing inventory checks on everything valuable. They use comment cards, well-placed mirrors, and sometimes even hidden cameras and spies to keep up this surveillance. We are controlled, monitored, and under threat constantly. Time at work in a typical restaurant is totalitarian.

But no totalitarian regime survives by coercion alone.

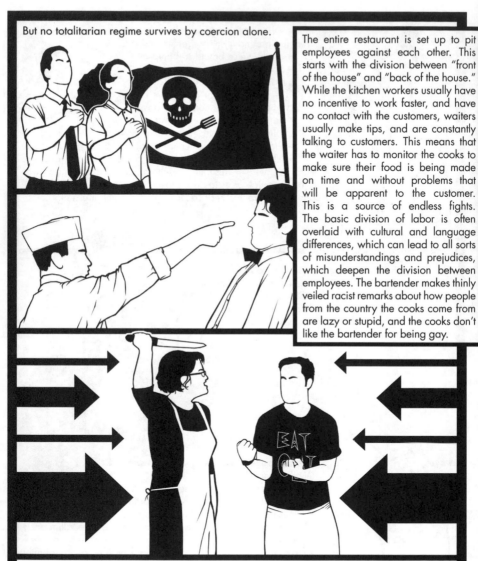

The entire restaurant is set up to pit employees against each other. This starts with the division between "front of the house" and "back of the house." While the kitchen workers usually have no incentive to work faster, and have no contact with the customers, waiters usually make tips, and are constantly talking to customers. This means that the waiter has to monitor the cooks to make sure their food is being made on time and without problems that will be apparent to the customer. This is a source of endless fights. The basic division of labor is often overlaid with cultural and language differences, which can lead to all sorts of misunderstandings and prejudices, which deepen the division between employees. The bartender makes thinly veiled racist remarks about how people from the country the cooks come from are lazy or stupid, and the cooks don't like the bartender for being gay.

Then in the front and the back of the house, there is a top and bottom. The employees who make more and who do more skilled work look down on the others and sometimes order them around or treat them like children. The bussers and dishwashers resent the workers who make more money than them, and want to move up. Especially among the wait-staff, management fosters an atmosphere of competition. We compare how much we sold at the end of the night, and try to sell more of this or that wine or entrée. On a slow night we try to get the hostess to seat people in our sections. On a busy one we try to get her to seat "problem tables" in other waiter's sections.

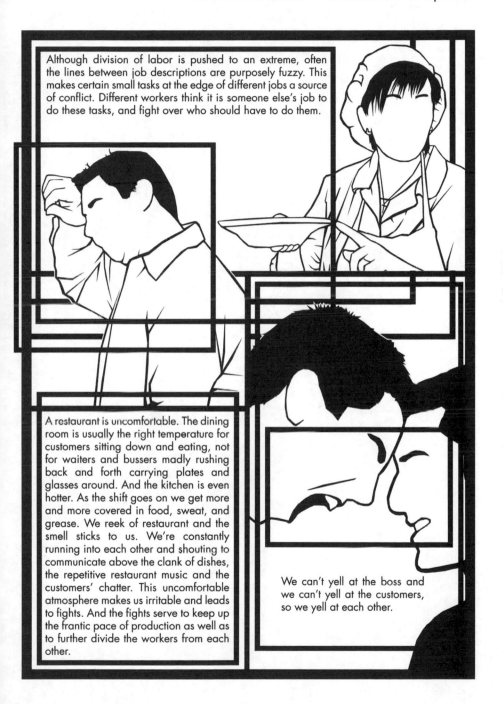

Although division of labor is pushed to an extreme, often the lines between job descriptions are purposely fuzzy. This makes certain small tasks at the edge of different jobs a source of conflict. Different workers think it is someone else's job to do these tasks, and fight over who should have to do them.

A restaurant is uncomfortable. The dining room is usually the right temperature for customers sitting down and eating, not for waiters and bussers madly rushing back and forth carrying plates and glasses around. And the kitchen is even hotter. As the shift goes on we get more and more covered in food, sweat, and grease. We reek of restaurant and the smell sticks to us. We're constantly running into each other and shouting to communicate above the clank of dishes, the repetitive restaurant music and the customers' chatter. This uncomfortable atmosphere makes us irritable and leads to fights. And the fights serve to keep up the frantic pace of production as well as to further divide the workers from each other.

We can't yell at the boss and we can't yell at the customers, so we yell at each other.

33

HOW A RESTAURANT
IS TAKEN APART

"Communism is for us not a state of affairs which is to be established, an ideal to which reality [will] have to adjust itself. We call communism the real movement which abolishes the present state of things. The conditions of this movement result from the premises now in existence."

Karl Marx

prole.info

WHAT THE WORKER WANTS

"Nothing is more alien to a strike than its end."

François Martin

With few exceptions, the workers in a restaurant want one thing more than anything else: to no longer be workers in a restaurant.

This doesn't mean we want to be unemployed. It means that restaurant work is an alienating and miserable way to make a living. We are forced to be there. Work does not feel like part of our lives. We feel like ourselves when we're not at work.

The fact that restaurant workers hate the work is obvious to the point of being a cliché. In most restaurants you can find people who "aren't really restaurant workers." They're actors, or writers, or musicians, or graphic designers. They're just working in a restaurant until they can save up some money and start up a business of their own, or until they get through school and can get a "real job." One way we try to escape from work is by quitting, hoping another restaurant will be better. Restaurant work has a very high turnover. Often the majority of employees in a restaurant have only been working there for a few months. Of course, whatever our illusions, most of us just keep moving from restaurant job to restaurant job, from bistro to bar and grill to lounge to diner to café.

This doesn't mean we have no pride. Anyone who is forced to do something over and over and over and over and over again has to take some minor interest in it or go crazy. Anyone who works in restaurants long enough can't help but take a little pride in all the knowledge they acquire about food, wine, and human behavior. Still, aside from a handful of chefs in very expensive restaurants, the only people who are really proud to be restaurant workers are the boss's pets, who are usually shunned by the rest of the workers.

But the rejection of our condition as restaurant workers is not simply a conscious preference. Often the workers who have the highest expectations, who are most interested in the food service industry, or who have the least hatred for the work, come into serious conflicts with the boss. They have greater illusions and greater surprise and indignation when they come into contact with the miserable reality of the restaurant. A restaurant is a boring, uncomfortable, stressful, repetitive, alienating, hierarchical machine for pumping out surplus value. Even the obsequious waiter who is always hanging around complimenting the boss and suggesting ways to better run the restaurant will one day get into a heated argument and quit when the boss blatantly treats him like a subordinate. Ironically, it is often those that openly recognize the miserable position they're in that last longest in restaurant jobs.

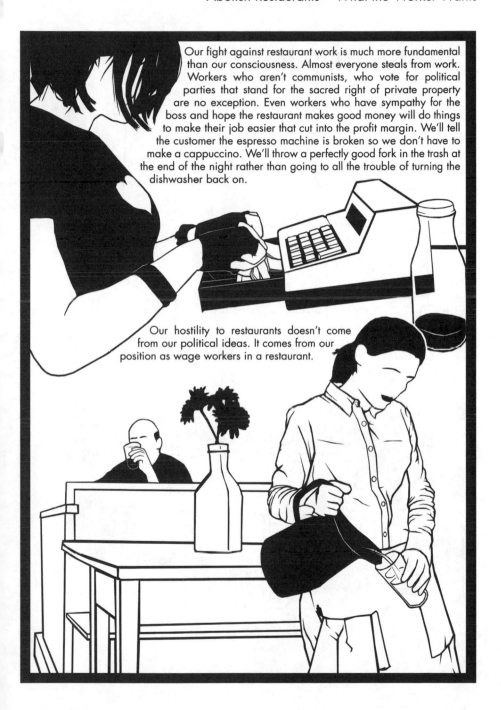

Our fight against restaurant work is much more fundamental than our consciousness. Almost everyone steals from work. Workers who aren't communists, who vote for political parties that stand for the sacred right of private property are no exception. Even workers who have sympathy for the boss and hope the restaurant makes good money will do things to make their job easier that cut into the profit margin. We'll tell the customer the espresso machine is broken so we don't have to make a cappuccino. We'll throw a perfectly good fork in the trash at the end of the night rather than going to all the trouble of turning the dishwasher back on.

Our hostility to restaurants doesn't come from our political ideas. It comes from our position as wage workers in a restaurant.

WORK GROUPS

"People drawn together within the same workplace talk with each other far more than those in the same hundred block of the same avenue."

Stan Weir

The workplace is set up not only to produce money for the boss, but also to produce restaurant workers who are isolated from each other, in competition with each other, prejudiced against each other, afraid for our jobs, and who only look for individual solutions to our problems. But this is only an ideal towards which management aspires. They are never completely successful because our activity tends to push in the opposite direction.

Restaurants bring us together with other restaurant workers in the same workplace. The work process itself requires that we cooperate and communicate with other workers. We pass plates back and forth. We explain food and drink orders. We figure out which tables need to be pressured to pay and leave to make room for upcoming reservations.

These conversations lead to more interesting ones. Everyone is looking for ways to make the work less boring or stressful. We joke around, deep fry candybars, juggle fruit, drum on the washing machine, and make fun of the customers.

This joking around leads to more serious cooperation. We spend a lot of time with our co-workers and learn a lot about each other. In between rushes we talk about our problems at work, in our personal life, with the immigration authorities. We are no longer a collection of separated individuals. We form informal groups of workers on the job which are capable of acting together. We go out for a drink after work. We cover each other's asses at work.

These work groups then set the general work culture of the restaurant. If we are weak, the culture of the restaurant can come pretty close to the ideal of bigoted, separated individuals, and the work is absolutely miserable. In this case, our desire to escape from work may also be a desire to escape from our co-workers. If we are strong, we can make the work a lot less miserable. When the boss isn't looking, the cooks will make food for the front-end staff, and they will steal drinks for the kitchen. We'll warn each other when the boss or the manager is coming around, and make fun of them when they're gone.

Since the work groups are based in the work process itself, the workers who take the lead in their formation and who set the work culture tend to be those that know the work process best. This can be the people who have worked at a particular restaurant the longest, or the people who have worked in the food service industry the longest. Often the easiest time to foster a healthy cynicism in a co-worker is when you're training them.

The glue that holds these informal work groups together is a struggle against the work. When we joke around when we're supposed to be working, or shit-talk the boss, or cut corners to make the work easier, or steal from work together, we create trust, complicity, and a culture of watching out for each other. This community of struggle cuts into profit-making, but it also tends to break down the divisions and hierarchies created by the production process. It is the basis for any broader fight against management.

The fact that work groups and the cultures they create are based in the work process means that the boss can undermine these groups by changing the work process. He can introduce a computer system to send orders to the kitchen to cut down on communication. He can change people's shifts so they work with a manager and therefore increase surveillance. He can change people's job description so they have some management duties and therefore change their sympathies. He can introduce comment cards, give or take away employee meals, add inventory duties, or just fire people. By changing the shape of the restaurant he can change the patterns of communication, socialization and cut down on resistance. The new shape then forms the basis for new work groups and new resistance. Generally speaking, the more conscious our solidarity has become, the more difficult it is to undermine.

The boss has the production process, money, the weight of prejudice, custom, isolation, inertia, and ultimately the law and the police on his side.

We only have each other.

WORKERS, MANAGEMENT, AND WORKER-MANAGEMENT

"Class society has a tremendous resilience, a great capacity to cope with 'subversion' to make icons of its iconoclasts, to draw sustenance from those who would throttle it."

Maurice Brinton

Our struggle against restaurant work is also a struggle against the way the work is set up—against the division of labor and the hierarchy at work. At the most basic level, we often take an interest in the jobs of other workers. In slow times, a bored waitress will prepare simple foods in the kitchen, while the dishwasher asks questions about the difference between different kinds of wines. The fact that the work process is so chopped up and specialized feels strange and unnatural to us, and we want to go beyond it. In order to form any kind of work groups, we have to treat each other as equals. This starts to undermine the divisions between skilled and unskilled and the hierarchy within the workers.

In any restaurant the workers have to be able to manage the work themselves to a large extent. We have to be able to prioritize tasks, as well as communicate and coordinate with other workers. In smaller restaurants the boss will sometimes even leave and we will have to manage everything ourselves. This means that our resentment towards the job often takes the form of a critique of how the restaurant is managed. We'll complain that the restaurant owner "has no class" for buying cheap ingredients or for serving near-rotten food. We make comments about how if we managed the place, things would be different. We develop our own ideas about how food should be cooked and served, and about how much things should cost.

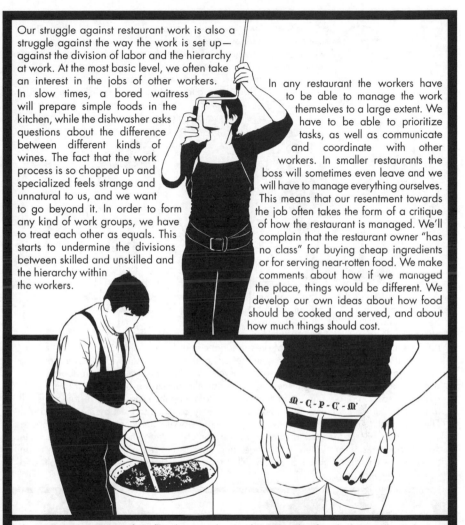

This is a constant cause of conflict, but it is also easily co-opted. Often the boss will simply give in to our desire to run things ourselves. The more disorganized and inefficient the restaurant, the more likely this is to happen. He'll let the hostess deal with problem customers. He won't buy enough supplies or fix machinery, and we'll have to fix machines or bring in supplies ourselves. He'll leave a cook alone with 10 orders at once, or a waitress with 10 tables at once saying "You work it out." And we have to push ourselves instead of being pushed directly. In fact, part of being a good restaurant employee is having internalized the rhythm of production, and being able to push yourself hard enough that management doesn't have to push you. In these situations we try to help each other out and do bits and pieces of each other's jobs—our solidarity with our co-workers is used against us as a way to get us to work harder.

Some restaurant workers have made an ideology out of the struggle over the way the work is set up. They set up cooperative restaurants where there is no boss. They do the work as well as make the management decisions themselves. In these restaurants, the workers are no-longer under the arbitrary power of a boss. They often eliminate some of the division of labor and the worst aspects of customer service. They may sell vegan, vegetarian, organic, "fairly traded," or locally grown food.

At the same time, they forget that the division of labor is brought about because it helps make money more efficiently. The boss isn't an asshole for no reason. The boss is under a lot of pressure that comes from outside the restaurant. He has to keep his money in motion, making more money. He has to compete and make a profit, or his business won't survive. Workers in a collective restaurant, like some "mom-and-pop" small businesses, have not eliminated the boss. They have merely rolled the position of boss and worker into one. No matter their ideals, the restaurant is still trapped within the economy. The restaurant can only continue to exist by making a profit. The work is still stressful and repetitive, only now the workers are themselves the managers. They have to enforce the work on themselves and on each other. This means that workers in self-managed restaurants often work longer and harder and are paid even less than those in regular restaurants. Either that or the self-managed restaurants don't make a profit and don't survive very long.

More common than self-management is that management replies to workers' struggle by trying to create some kind of community within the restaurant. They know that workers brought together in a restaurant will form groups. Instead of fostering isolation and prejudice, they foster community—a community that includes the restaurant management. This is especially common in small restaurants, where employees may even be related to each other and management. The boss may explain how tough business is, especially for a small independent restaurant like his. The boss may be gay or a woman or from an ethnic minority and try to create some kind of community based on that identity. The restaurant may not sell certain brands, they might only sell "fairly traded," organic, or vegetarian foods.

Whatever the community, the function is to smooth over the class struggle. The idea is that instead of simply standing up for our own interests, which would naturally bring us into conflict with management, we should take management's point of view into account. We may have some problems, but our boss also has problems, and we have to come to some kind of compromise—a compromise that ends up with us working for them. Unlike tipping, this is a purely ideological way of tying workers to the work, and tends to be less effective. Still, management never has more control over the workers than when the workers believe they're working for a good cause.

With self-management, as with the community which includes management, we are supposed to enforce the work on ourselves and on each other. Both are a response to our struggle against our situation that ultimately just creates a greater form of alienation. Our problem with restaurants is much deeper than just how they are managed. And we can't solve our problems by working with management.

47

UNIONS

"The representation of the working class has become an enemy of the working class."

Guy Debord

As our struggles against restaurants become stronger and we look for more visible, above-ground ways of fighting, unions present themselves. Generally speaking, restaurants are now, and have always been non-union. Where unions have existed, they have followed the same path as unions in other industries, only less successfully.

Restaurants often have a very high turnover. People only last a few months. They employ lots of young people who are only looking for part-time or temporary employment. Restaurant jobs aren't seen as desirable, and people are always looking to move to a better job. This makes the creation of stable unions very difficult. But this state of affairs is as much a result of an unorganized industry as it is a cause. Many industries were like this before unions took hold. In heavily unionized industries, employers have been forced to give up the power to hire, fire, and change job descriptions at will. Workers entrench themselves and defend this inflexibility.

Restaurants, like many areas of the service industry, have to go where the demand is. They can't be concentrated in industrial corridors in one area of a country. Restaurant workers tend to be spread out, working for thousands of small restaurant bosses, instead of a few large ones. This means we have a thousand different grievances and it's not easy to organize together.

Also, although there are restaurants everywhere, and they account for a large amount of economic activity, they aren't a decisive sector. If a restaurant goes on strike, this doesn't create a ripple effect disrupting other areas of the economy. If truck drivers go on strike, not only is the trucking company's business disrupted, but grocery stores, malls, and everyone else that depends on the goods that the truck drivers ship are also disrupted. If a restaurant goes on strike, the main effect is that other restaurants in the area will do a bit better business. This puts us in a weak position, and means that employers are less likely to agree to pay higher wages in return for guaranteed production as they may be in other more decisive industries.

Early restaurant workers fought for the 10-hour day, the 6-day week and an end to the "vampire system" of hiring (where restaurant workers went to a café and were set up with a job by spending a lot of money on drinks or by paying a bribe to the café owner). These workers' struggles took many different forms. There were elite craft unions which only tried to unionize waiters and cooks. There were industrial unions which would unionize anyone who worked in a restaurant or hotel in the same union. Some of these, such as the Industrial Workers of the World, even refused to sign contracts with the employer. There were also actions by restaurant workers not in unions or in any organization at all.

Employers first fought the unions, hiring scabs, using hired thugs and police to beat up workers on strike—fearing any representation of the workers would cut into their profits. As unions grew, employers were forced to bargain with them. Employers used this to their own advantage.

Joining a union became a protected right in many places. Union bargaining procedures were written into law. Workers representatives were recognized. A whole series of gains were turned on their heads.

Union dues were taken directly out of all workers paychecks. This was meant to make it easier to organize all the workers in a particular enterprise, but it also served to make the union less dependent on the union members. The unions developed a bureaucracy of paid staff and organizers. Having paid staff meant that the union activists and negotiators couldn't be harassed or fired by management. It also meant that they couldn't be easily controlled by workers. Paid staff aren't on the job. They have interests different from and at times in direct conflict with the workers. The contract, which was fought for so hard, often included real gains for the workers. Employers gave in to higher wages, more security, and better conditions in return for a no-strike guarantee during the length of a contract. Management agreed to pay more, and to give up some control, in order to maintain uninterrupted production. The union was then put in the position of enforcing the contract on the workers.

The unions became institutionalized negotiators between management and the workers. They fight to keep this position. They organize workers and mobilize us against management in controlled ways. They need dues money and contracts. But when workers' discontent gets outside their control, they fight it. They are bureaucracies trying to maintain themselves. Workers today may want to be in unions, the same way we want a good lawyer, but we don't see the unions as our own and we are often as skeptical of them as we are of politicians or leftist sects.

Mothers For Fines and Jail Time

serve the people

The arc of the union movement isn't just something that happened once in history. It is a dynamic we can see in union struggles over and over again. Time and again new generations of workers build up unions. Grassroots caucuses change the unions from within. The new radical union leaders replace the old union hacks, but when put in the same position, under the same pressures, they react the same way. In this way the bureaucracy is rejuvenated. Sometimes the fight to "reform our union" even takes the place of the fight against the boss. All the while production continues quite profitably.

Don't hate the mediator. Be the mediator.

All these things can be seen in restaurant unions, but not as dramatically as in other unions. More often than not, restaurant owners have been successful in simply crushing unionization campaigns.

Unions are built by workers, but are not the workers. The unions represent workers as workers within the work process. While they may call strikes and even break the law, their starting and ending point is us at work. They can at times and in certain places help us win better wages and conditions. As often as not they oppose even low-level struggles. And ultimately they get in our way.

Restaurant unions need there to be restaurants. We don't.

A WORLD WITHOUT RESTAURANTS

"It is only when the routine daily struggle of the class
explodes into violent activity against the bourgeoisie (the throwing of
a foreman out of the window, the conflict with the police on the mass picket line,
etc.), activities which require an overt exercise of their creative energies, that the
workers feel themselves as human. As a result, the return from the picket line
to the covert class struggle is even more frustrating than if the strike had never
taken place. The molecular development of these offensives and retreats can
only explode in the revolution which will enable the working class to employ its
creative energies not only in smashing the old relations of production but also in
establishing new social ties of a positive and creative character."

Ria Stone

The conditions that create intense work and intense boredom in a restaurant are the same that create "law and order" and development in some countries, and wars, famines, and poverty in others.

The logic that pits workers against each other, or ties us together with management in a restaurant, is the same logic behind the rights of citizens and the deportation of "illegals."

The world that needs democracies, dictatorships, terrorists, and police also needs fine dining, fast food, waiters, and cooks.

The pressures we feel in everyday life are the same that erupt in the crisis and disasters that interrupt everyday life. We feel the weight of our bosses' money wanting to move and expand.

A restaurant is set up by and for the movement of capital. We are brought into the production process and created as restaurant workers by this movement. But we make the food and make it sell. The movement of our bosses' money is nothing more than our activity made into something which controls us. In order to make life bearable, we fight against this process, and the bosses who profit from it.

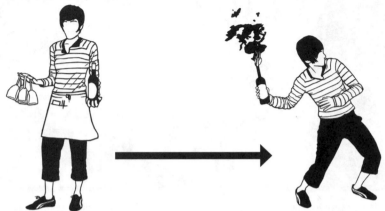

The impulse to fight against work and management is immediately collective. As we fight against the conditions of our own lives, we see that other people are doing the same. To get anywhere we have to fight side by side. We begin to break down the divisions between us and prejudices, hierarchies, and nationalisms begin to be undermined. As we build trust and solidarity, we grow more daring and combative. More becomes possible. We get more organized, more confident, more disruptive, and more powerful.

Restaurants aren't strategic. They aren't the hub of value-creation in the capitalist economy. They are just one battlefield in an international class war that we're all a part of whether we like it or not.

In Spain in July of 1936, millions of workers armed themselves and took over their workplaces. Restaurant workers took over the restaurants, abolished tips, and used restaurants to feed the workers' militias going off to fight the fascist armies. But the workers in arms had not gone far enough, and had left the state intact. The Communist Party soon took over the government and the police, jailed or shot the radical workers and reversed most of the gains of the revolution. Within a year, restaurants were almost back to normal, and waiters were receiving tips again, this time from Party leaders.

Every time we attack this system but don't destroy it, it changes, and in turn changes us and the terrain of the next fight. Gains are turned against us, and we are stuck back in the same situation—at work. The bosses try to keep us looking for individual solutions, or solutions within an individual workplace or an individual trade. The only way we can free ourselves is to broaden and deepen our fight. We involve workers from other workplaces, industries, and regions. We attack more and more fundamental things. The desire to destroy restaurants becomes the desire to destroy the conditions that create restaurants.

We aren't just fighting for representation in or control over the production process. Our fight isn't against the act of chopping vegetables or washing dishes or pouring beer or even serving food to other people. It is with the way all these acts are brought together in a restaurant, separated from other acts, become part of the economy, and are used to expand capital. The starting and ending point of this process is a society of capitalists and people forced to work for them. We want an end to this. We want to destroy the production process, as something outside and against us. We're fighting for a world where our productive activity fulfills a need and is an expression of our lives, not forced on us in exchange for a wage—a world where we produce for each other directly and not in order to sell to each other. The struggle of restaurant workers is ultimately for a world without restaurants or workers.

This is the direction we push every day.

We need to push harder and better.

We can't let anything stand in our way.

CAPITALIST
SOCIETY

Inspired by the old I.W.W.
**"PYRAMID of CAPITALIST
SYSTEM**," the following spread is a
portrayal of class society as it appears
to us today. The whirlwind of market
forces encircle and shape society, operating
through our activity, yet behind our backs.
People at different levels of the modern capitalist
pyramid enjoy it or defend it or cope with it or
fight it or get drunk to forget about their place in it.

Designed in collaboration with wapiti.se.

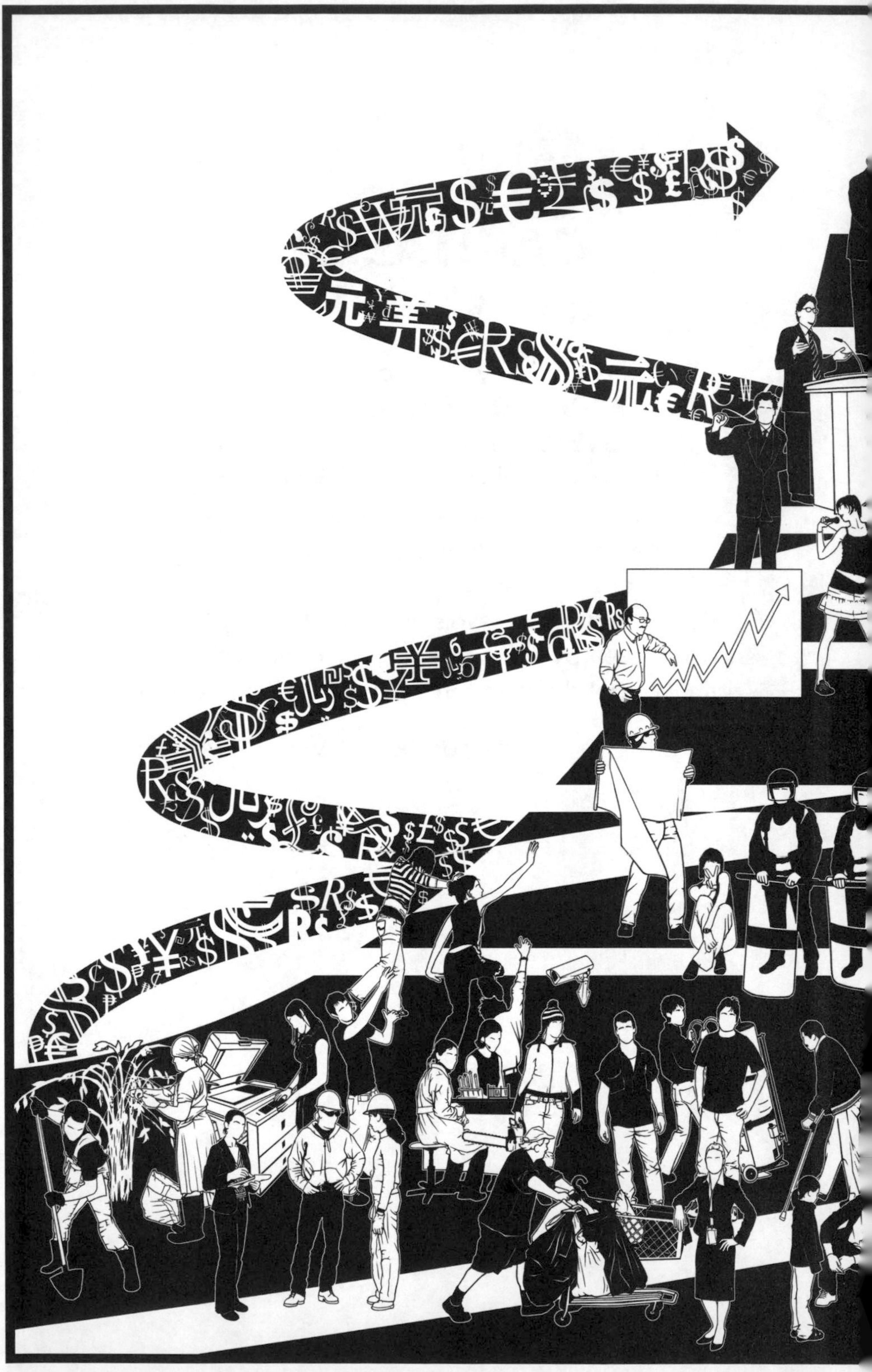

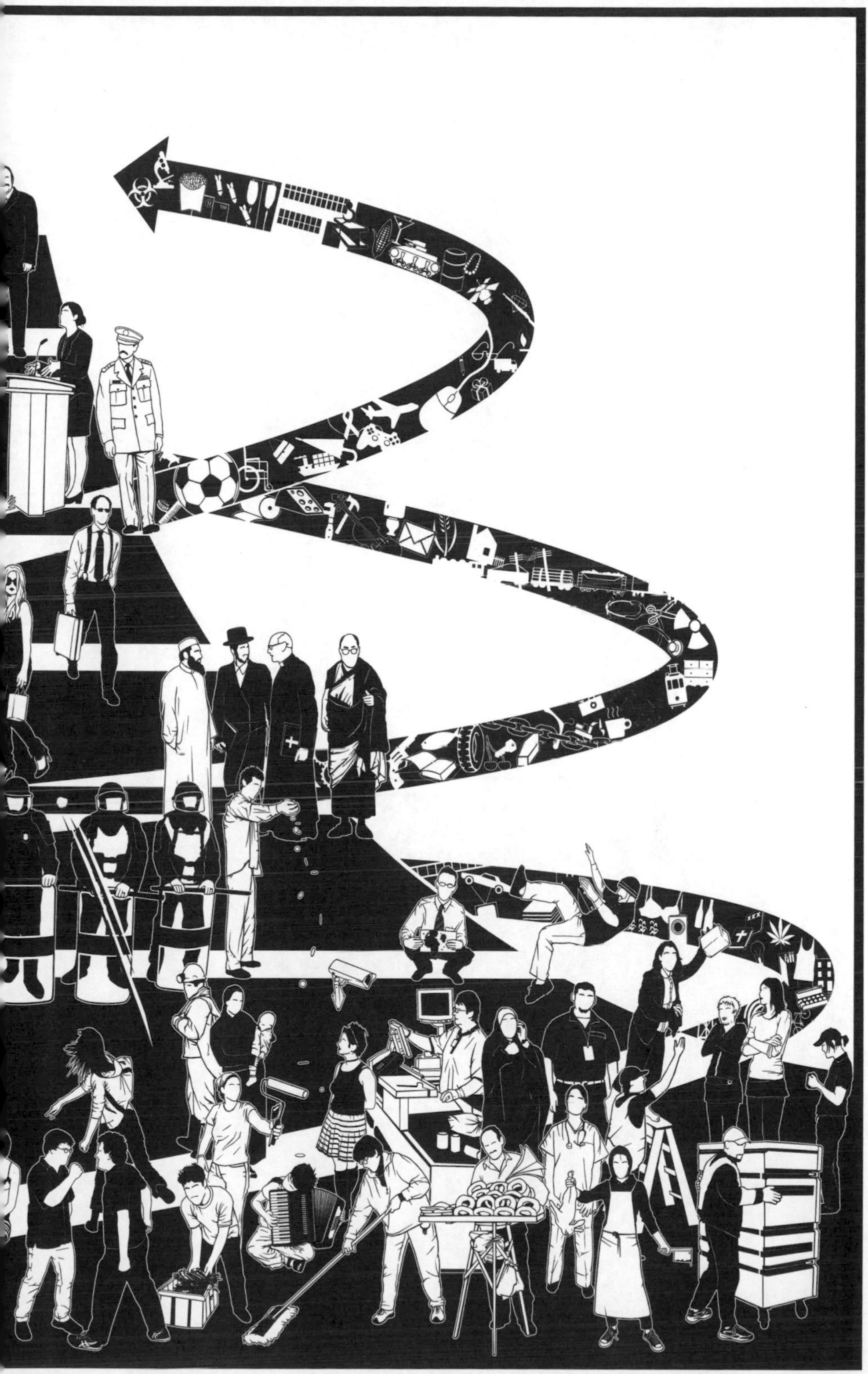

work

community

politics

war

"Everyone is asked their opinion about every detail in order to prevent them from having one about the totality."

Raoul Vaneigem

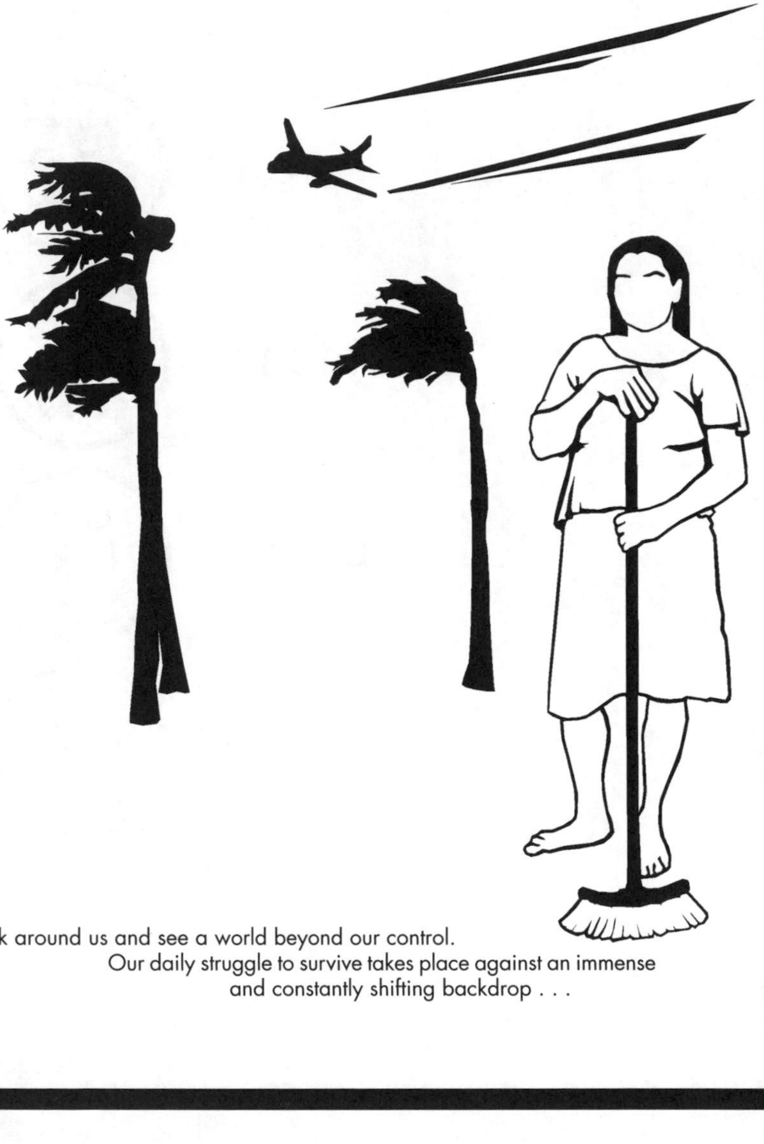

We look around us and see a world beyond our control.
Our daily struggle to survive takes place against an immense
and constantly shifting backdrop . . .

. . . moving from natural disaster to terrorist attack . . . from new diet to new famine . . . from celebrity sex scandal to political corruption scandal . . . from religious war to economic miracle . . . from tantalizing new advertisement to clichés on TV complaining about the government . . . from suggestions on how to be the ideal lover to suggestions on how to keep sports fans from rioting . . . from new police shootings to new health problems . . .

The same processes are at work everywhere . . . in democratic and in totalitarian governments . . . in corporations and in mom-and-pop businesses . . . in cheeseburgers and in tofu . . . in opera, in country music and in hip hop . . . in every country and in every language . . . in prisons, in schools, in hospitals, in factories, in office towers, in war zones, and in grocery stores. Something is feeding off our lives and spitting back images of them in our faces.

That something is the product of our own activity . . . our everyday working lives sold hour after hour, week after week, generation after generation. We don't have property or a business we can make money from, so we are forced to sell our time and energy to someone else. We are the modern-day working class—the proles.

WORK

"Capital is dead labour, that, vampire-like, only lives by sucking living labour, and lives the more, the more labour it sucks."

Karl Marx

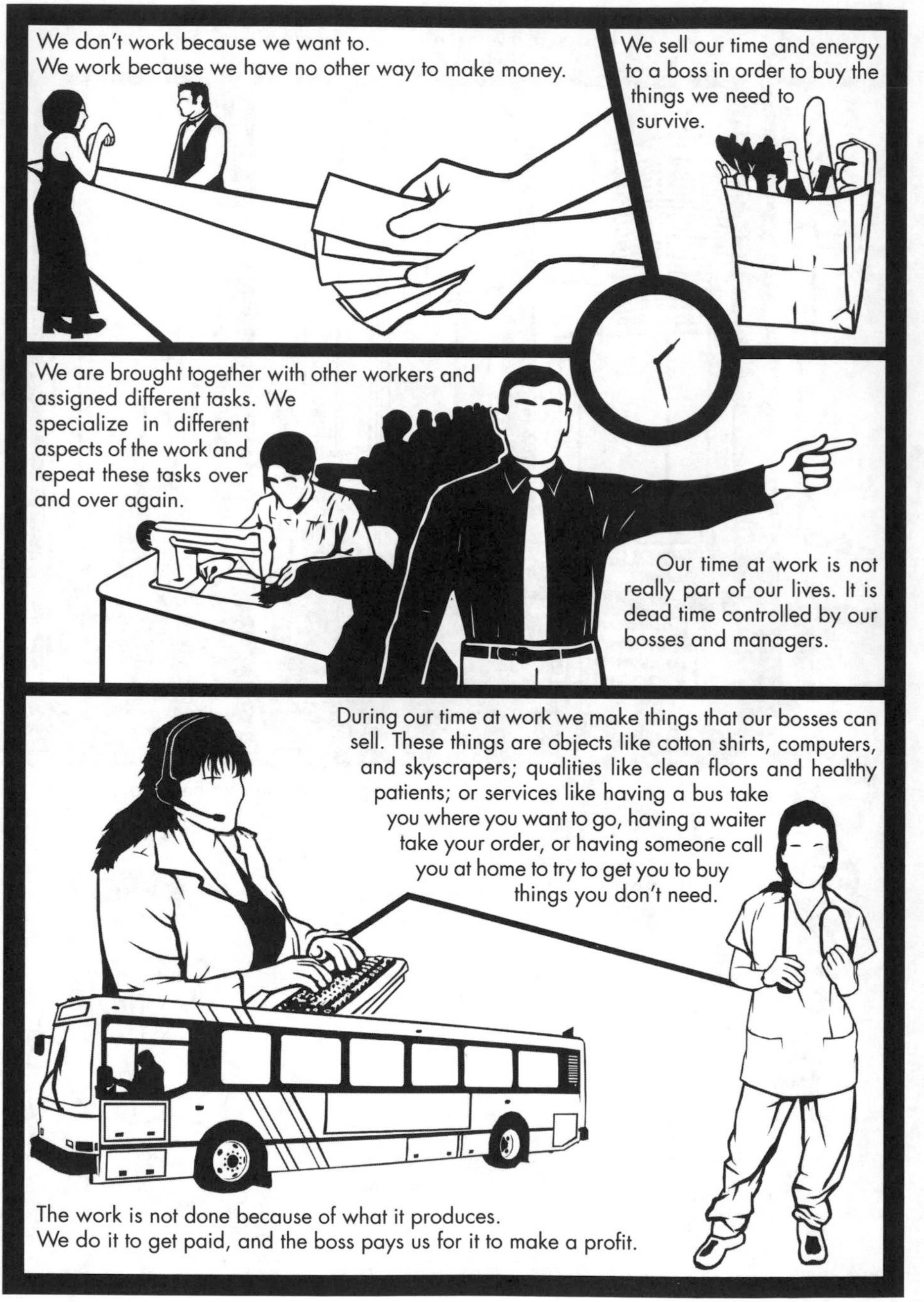
We don't work because we want to.
We work because we have no other way to make money.
We sell our time and energy to a boss in order to buy the things we need to survive.
We are brought together with other workers and assigned different tasks. We specialize in different aspects of the work and repeat these tasks over and over again.
Our time at work is not really part of our lives. It is dead time controlled by our bosses and managers.
During our time at work we make things that our bosses can sell. These things are objects like cotton shirts, computers, and skyscrapers; qualities like clean floors and healthy patients; or services like having a bus take you where you want to go, having a waiter take your order, or having someone call you at home to try to get you to buy things you don't need.
The work is not done because of what it produces.
We do it to get paid, and the boss pays us for it to make a profit.

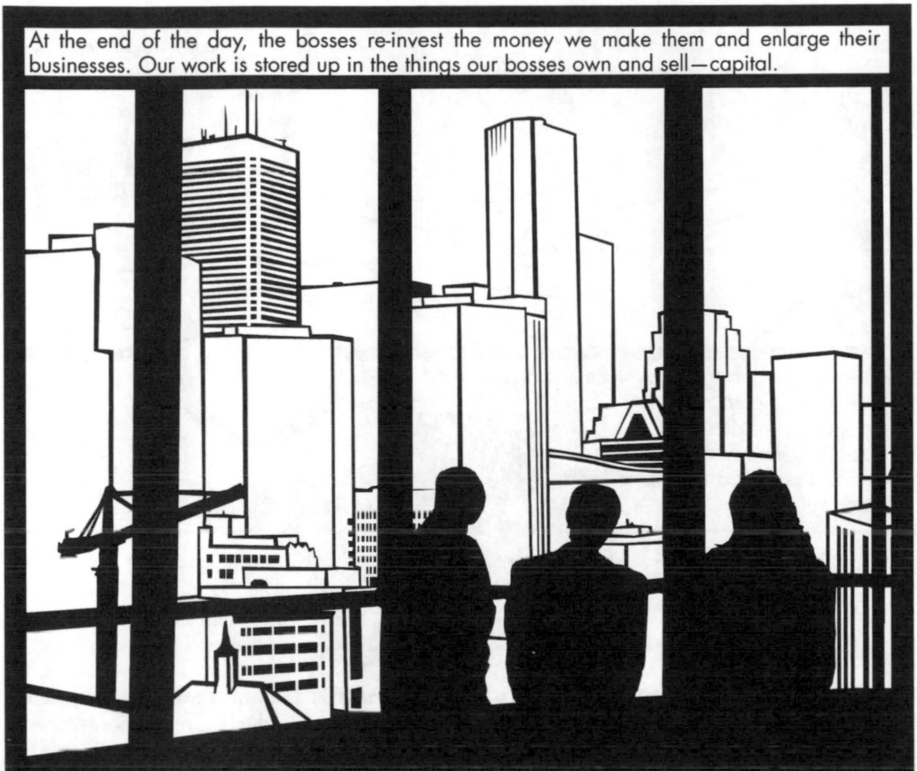
At the end of the day, the bosses re-invest the money we make them and enlarge their businesses. Our work is stored up in the things our bosses own and sell—capital.

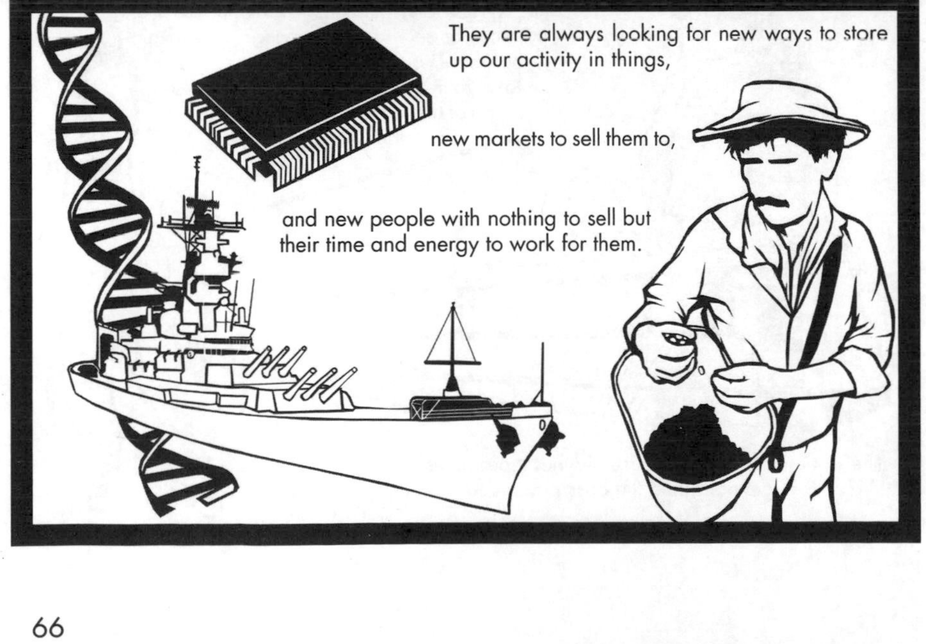
They are always looking for new ways to store up our activity in things,
new markets to sell them to,
and new people with nothing to sell but their time and energy to work for them.

What we get from work is enough money to pay for rent, food, clothes, and beer—enough to keep us coming back to work. When we're not at work, we spend time traveling to or from work, preparing for work, resting up because we're exhausted from work, or getting drunk to forget about work.

The only thing worse than work is not having it. Then we waste our weeks away looking for work, without getting paid for it. If welfare is available, it is a pain-in-the-ass to get and is never as much as working. The constant threat of unemployment is what keeps us going to work every day.

And our work is the basis of this society. The power our bosses get from it expands every time we work. It is the dominant force in every country in the world.

At work we are under the control of our bosses, and of the markets they sell to. But an invisible hand imposes a work-like discipline and pointlessness on the rest of our lives as well. Life seems like a kind of show we watch from the outside but have no control over.

All sorts of other activities tend to become as alienating, boring, and stressful as work: housework, schoolwork, leisure. That's capitalism.

ANTI-WORK

"Of course, the capitalists are very much satisfied with the capitalist system. Why shouldn't they be? They get rich by it."

Alexander Berkman

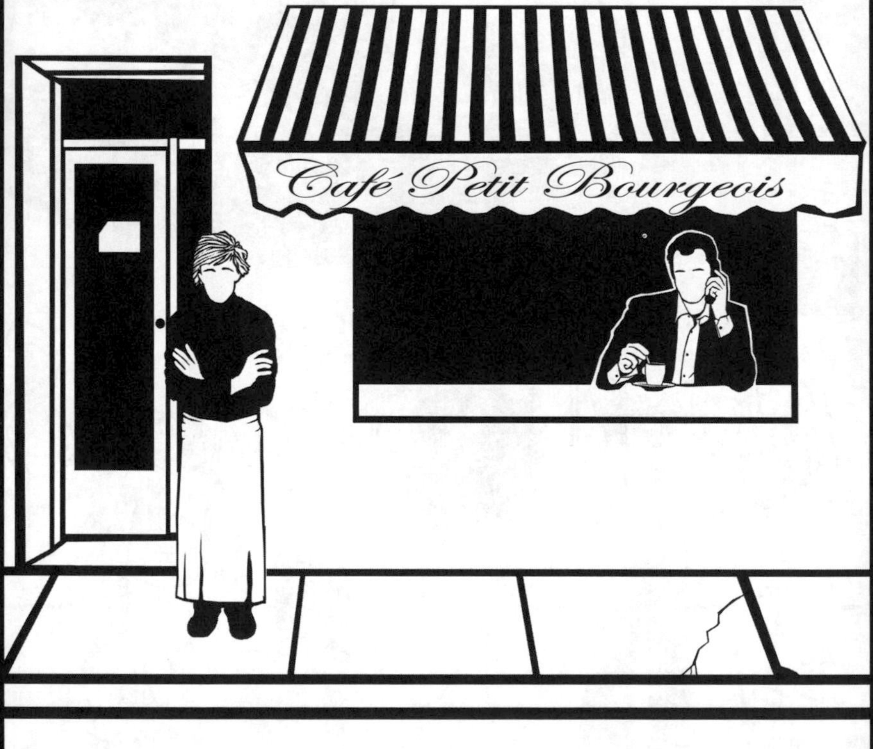
Café Petit Bourgeois

Work is experienced very differently depending on which side of it you're on. For our bosses, work is the way that they get their money to make more money. For us, work is a miserable way to survive. The less they pay us, the less we make. The faster they can get us to work, the harder we have to work.

Our interests are opposed, and there is a constant struggle between bosses and workers at work—and in the rest of the society based on work. The more we pay in rent or bus fare, the more we have to work to pay our rent or bus fare.

Ceci n'est pas une camera.

The current state of wages, benefits, hours, and working conditions as well as politics, art, and technology is a result of the current state of this class struggle. Simply standing up for our own interests in this struggle is the starting point of undermining capitalism.

COMMUNITY

"Well, it is about time that every rebel wakes up to the fact that 'the people' and the working class have nothing in common."

Joe Hill

Civilization is deeply divided. Most of us spend most of our time working and are mostly poor, while the owners, who are mostly rich, manage and profit off our work. All the communities and institutions of society are built up around this basic division. There are racial, cultural, and language divisions and communities. There is division and community around sex and age. There is the community of the nation and citizenship, as well as the division between nations and those with and without citizenship. We are divided and united around religion and ideology. We are brought together to buy and sell on the market.

prole.info

Some of these identities have been around for millennia. Some are a direct result of the way we work today. But they are all now organized around capital. They are all used to help our bosses accumulate more of our dead time stored up in things, and to keep the basic division of this society from tearing it apart.

Poor people from one country can be made to identify with their bosses from the same country and can be made to fight poor people from other countries. Workers have a harder time organizing a strike with workers who look different and speak a different language, especially if one group thinks it's better than the other.

These divisions and communities are reflected in and reflect the division of labor at work.

74

While these divisions and exclusive communities are being pushed on us from one side, an all-inclusive human community is sold to us from the other. This community is just as imaginary and false. It denies the basic division of society.

Business owners run the government and the media, the schools and prisons, the welfare offices and the police. We have our lives run by them. The newspapers and television put forward their view of the world. Schools teach about the great (or unfortunate) history of their society and produce a spectrum of graduates and dropouts fit for different kinds of work. The government provides services to keep their society running smoothly.

And when all else fails, they have the police, the prisons, and the army.

This is not our community.

ANTI-COMMUNITY

"Such power as the bourgeoisie still possesses in this period resides in the proletariat's lack of autonomy and independence of spirit."

Anton Pannekoek

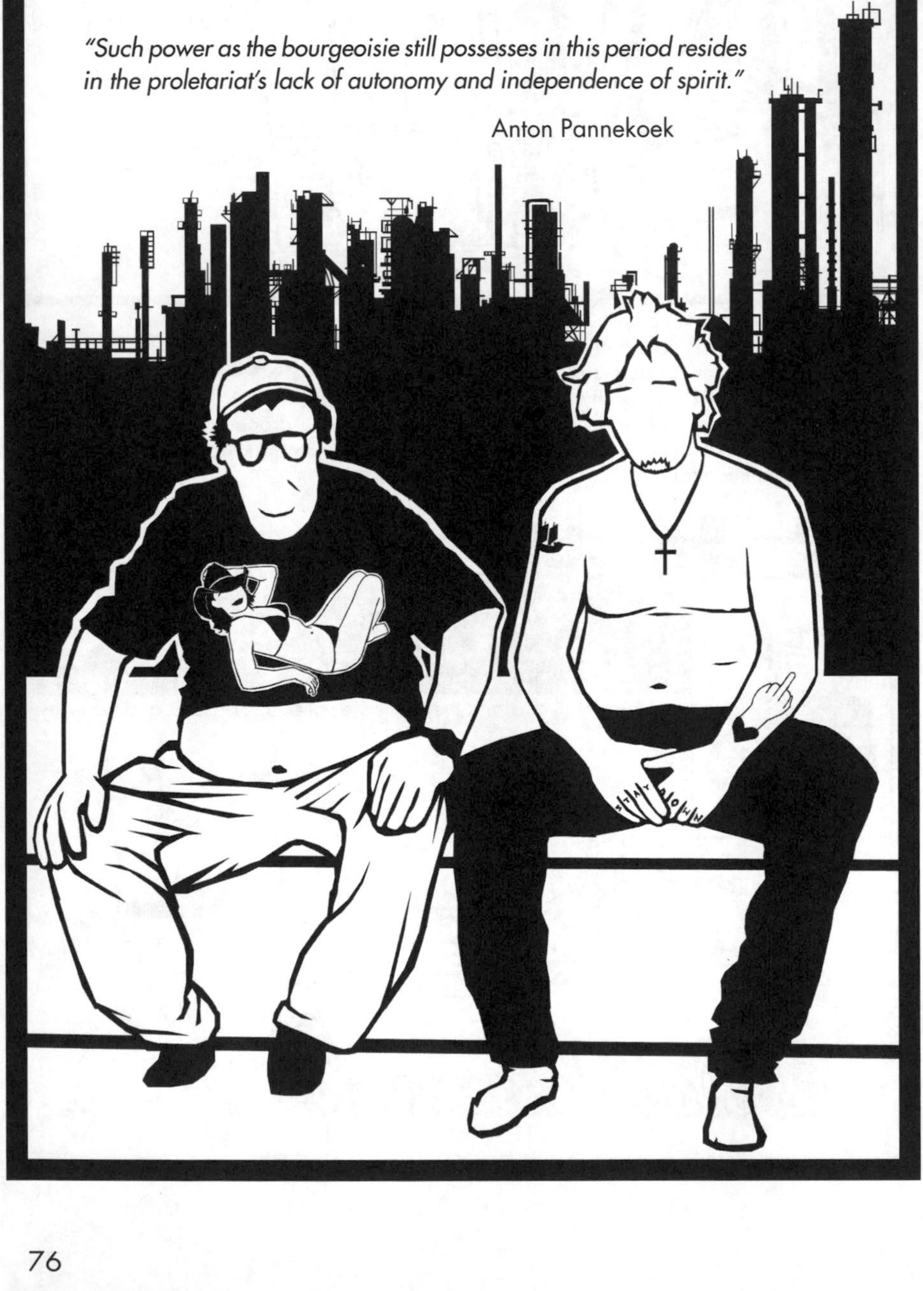
STAY
DOWN

They organize us against each other, but we can organize ourselves against them. The whole point of talking about class and "the proles" is to insist on the very basic way in which people from different "communities" have essentially similar experiences, and to show that people from the same "communities" should in fact hate each other. This is the starting point to fighting the existing communities. When we begin to fight for our own interests we see that others are doing the same thing. Prejudices fall away, and our anger is directed where it belongs.

We are not weak because we are divided. We are divided because we are weak.

The existing communities become irrelevant as they are attacked, and they are attacked by becoming irrelevant.

Racism and sexism are unappealing, when working men and women of different races are fighting their class enemies side by side. And that fight becomes more effective by involving people from different "communities."

prole.info

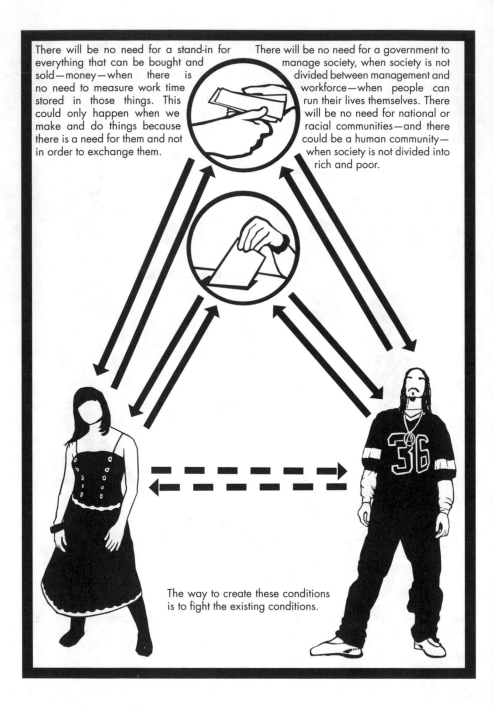

There will be no need for a stand-in for everything that can be bought and sold—money—when there is no need to measure work time stored in those things. This could only happen when we make and do things because there is a need for them and not in order to exchange them.

There will be no need for a government to manage society, when society is not divided between management and workforce—when people can run their lives themselves. There will be no need for national or racial communities—and there could be a human community—when society is not divided into rich and poor.

The way to create these conditions is to fight the existing conditions.

78

This tendency to create community by fighting against the conditions of our lives—and therefore against work, money, exchange, borders, nations, governments, police, religion, and race—has at times been called "communism."

POLITICS

"The more we are governed, the less we are free."

The Alarm

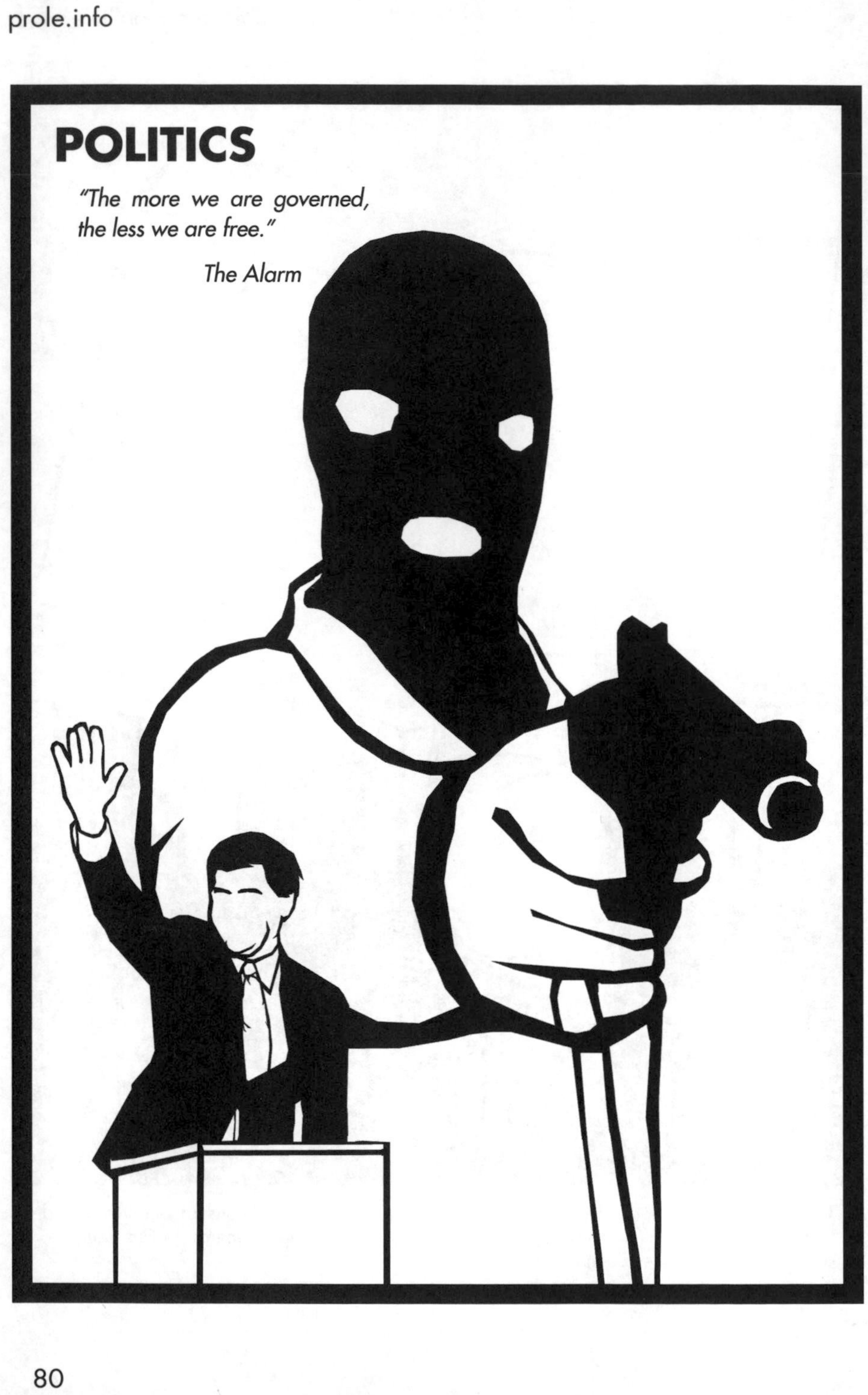

The government is the model for political activity. Politicians representing different countries, regions, or "communities" battle with each other. We are encouraged to support the leaders we disagree with least, and we're never really surprised when they screw us over.

All of a politician's working class background or radical ideals are worthless once they begin to govern. No matter who is in government, government has its own logic.

The fact that this society is divided into classes with opposing interests means that it is always at risk of tearing itself apart. The government is there to make sure that doesn't happen.

Whether the government is a dictatorship or a democracy, it holds all the guns and will use them against its own population to make sure that we keep going to work.

Not that long ago, an extremely unstable situation in a particular country could be diffused by nationalizing all of a country's industries, creating a police state, and calling it "communism." This kind of capitalism proved to be less efficient and less flexible than good old-fashioned free market capitalism. With the fall of the Soviet Union, there is no longer a Red Army to march in and stabilize countries in this way, and Communist parties around the world are becoming simple social democrats.

A working class political party is a contradiction in terms—not because the membership of a particular party can't be largely working class, but because the most it can do is give the working class a voice in politics. It lets our representatives put forward ideas on how our bosses should run this society—how they can make money and keep us under control. Whether they are advocating nationalization or privatization, more welfare or more police (or both), the programs of political parties are different strategies for managing capitalism.

Unfortunately, politics also exists outside of government. Community leaders, professional activists, and unions want to place themselves between workers and bosses and be the mediators, the negotiators, the means of communication, the representatives, and ultimately the peacemakers. They fight to keep this position. In order to do that, they need to mobilize the working class in controlled ways to put pressure on more business-oriented politicians, at the same time offering business a workforce that is ready to work. This means that they have to disperse us when we start to fight back. Sometimes they do this by negotiating concessions, other times by selling us out.

Politicians always call on us to vote, to sit back and let the organizer negotiate, to fall in line behind the leaders and the specialists in a kind of passive participation. These non-governmental politicians offer the government a way to maintain the status quo peacefully, and in return they get jobs managing our misery.

Political groups are bureaucratic. They tend to mirror the structures of work where activity is controlled from the outside. They create specialists in politics. They are built on a division between leaders and led, between representatives and represented, between organizers and organized. This is not a bad choice of how to set up organizations, to be remedied with a large dose of participatory democracy. It is a direct result of what political groups and activities are trying to do—to manage a part of capitalism.

The only thing that interests us about politics is its destruction.

ANTI-POLITICS

"Anarchism is not a beautiful utopia, nor an abstract philosophical idea, it is a social movement of the labouring masses."

Dyelo Truda Group

When we start to fight against the conditions of our lives, a completely different kind of activity appears. We do not look for a politician to come change things for us. We do it ourselves, with other working class people. Whenever this kind of working class resistance breaks out, politicians try to extinguish it in a flood of petitions, lobbying, and election campaigns. But when we are fighting for ourselves, our activity looks completely different from theirs. We take property away from landlords and use it for ourselves. We use militant tactics against our bosses and end up fighting with the police. We form groups where everyone takes part in the activity, and there is no division between leaders and followers. We do not fight for our leaders, for our bosses, or for our country. We fight for ourselves.

This is not the ultimate form of democracy. We are imposing our needs on society without debate—needs that are directly contrary to the interests and wishes of rich people everywhere. There is no way for us to speak on equal terms with this society.

This tendency of working class struggles to go outside and against the government and politics, and to create new forms of organization that do not put our faith in anything other than our own ability, has at times been called "anarchism."

WAR

"Let us devastate the avenues where the wealthy live."

Lucy Parsons

So we're in a war—a class war. There is no set of ideas, proposals, and organizational strategies that can bring victory. There is no solution outside of winning the war.

So long as they have the initiative, we are separated, and passive. Our response to the conditions of our lives is individual: quitting our jobs, moving to neighborhoods with cheaper rent, joining subcultures and gangs, suicide, buying lottery tickets, drug abuse and alcoholism, going to church.

Their world looks like the only possibility. Any hope for change is lived on an imaginary level— separated from our everyday lives. It's business as usual, with all the crisis and destruction that this implies.

When we go on the offensive we begin to recognize each other and to fight collectively. We use the ways that society depends on us to disrupt it. We strike, sabotage, riot, desert, mutiny, and take over property. We create organizations in order to amplify and coordinate our activities. All kinds of new possibilities open up.

BORN TO LOSE

FIGHT TO WIN

CAPITAL

those who make revolutions half way only dig their own graves

NO

NO WAR

NO WAR BUT THE CLASS WAR

NO WAR BUT THE CLASS WAR

NO WAR BUT THE CLASS WAR

We grow more daring and more aggressive in pursuing our own class interests. These do not lie in forming a new government or becoming the new boss. Our interests lie in ending our own way of life—and therefore the society that is based on that way of life.

We are the working class who want to abolish work and class. We are the community of people who want to tear the existing community apart. Our political program is to destroy politics. In order to do that, we have to push the subversive tendencies that exist today until we have completely remade society everywhere. This has at times been called "revolution."

About PM Press

politics • culture • art • fiction • music • film

PM Press was founded at the end of 2007 by a small collection of folks with decades of publishing, media, and organizing experience.

We seek to create radical and stimulating media to entertain, educate, and inspire. We aim to distribute these through every available channel with every available technology, whether that means you are seeing anarchist classics at our bookfair stalls; reading our latest vegan cookbook at the café; downloading geeky fiction e-books; or digging new music and timely videos from our website.

Contact us for direct ordering and questions about all PM Press releases, as well as manuscript submissions, review copy requests, foreign rights sales, author interviews, to book an author for an event, and to have PM Press attend your bookfair:

PM Press • PO Box 23912 • Oakland, CA 94623
510-658-3906 • info@pmpress.org • www.pmpress.org

FOPM: MONTHLY SUBSCRIPTION PROGRAM

Friends of PM allows you to directly help impact, amplify, and revitalize the discourse and actions of radical writers and artists. It provides us with a stable foundation to build upon our early successes and provides a much-needed subsidy for the materials that can't necessarily pay their own way. You can help make that happen—and receive every new title automatically delivered to your door once a month. And, we'll throw in a free T-shirt when you sign up.

Here are your options:
- **$30 a month:** Get all books and pamphlets plus 50% discount on all webstore purchases
- **$40 a month:** Get all PM Press releases (including CDs and DVDs) plus 50% discount on all webstore purchases
- **$100 a month:** Superstar—Everything plus PM merchandise, free downloads, and 50% discount on all webstore purchases

For those who can't afford $30 or more a month, we have **Sustainer Rates** at $15, $10 and $5. Sustainers get a free PM Press T-shirt and a 50% discount on all purchases from our website.

Your Visa or Mastercard will be billed once a month, until you tell us to stop. Or until our efforts succeed in bringing the revolution around. Or the financial meltdown of Capital makes plastic redundant. Whichever comes first.